The Mystery of the
Raddlesham Mumps

For Enid

Published by Scotland Street Press (SS Press Ltd)
100 Willowbrae Avenue
Edinburgh EH8 7HU

A CIP catalogue record for this book is available from the British Library

First published in Scotland in 2018 by
Scotland Street Press
scotlandstreetpress@gmail.com

ISBN: 978-1-910895-27-6 (paperback)
ISBN: 978-1-910895-26-9 (hardback)

Typeset by Hewer Text UK Ltd, Edinburgh
Printed by Bell & Bain in Glasgow, Scotland

Cover design by Angus Henderson using illustration by Julie Verhoeven

The Mystery of the
Raddlesham Mumps

Murray Lachlan Young

This book belongs to

Act 1.

Now welcome dear friend to this sinister tale
Welcome the wind and the brutalist hail
See the black mare in the blackest of plume
See the glass coach and the bleak floral bloom.

See the fine lace see the fluttering stole
See the twin coffins descending the hole
Chilling the marrow with famishing cold
Of a strange little boy: only seven years old.

Seven years old he was seven years old
Ripped like a lamb from the warmth of the fold
Britches of red with a curl in his hair
Thrust to the fore like a pig at a fair.

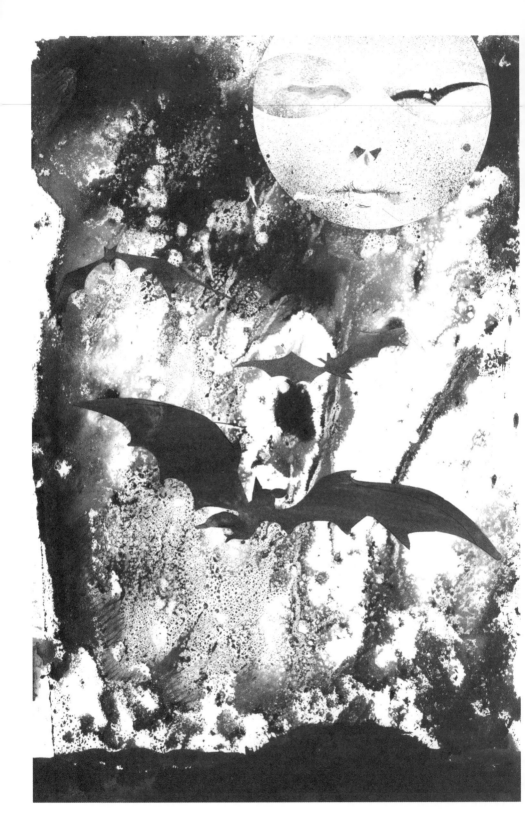

Down with them, down with them, down with them, down
Mother and father deep into the ground
And Crispin de Quincy de Faversham-Clumps
This day became master of Raddlesham Mumps.

Raddlesham Mumps was the seat of the Clumps
As ancient and strange as the old fairy tumps
Stacked high and wide like a mound of crow feather
With rumours the wallpaper held it together.

But ask the true story of Raddlesham Mumps
And ask for the fate of the Faversham-Clumps
Ask of the villagers what happened there
And meet with the murmurs of death and despair.

'Nothing will ever go right at the Mumps
'Nothing will ever go right for the Clumps
Ever since building on sacredest ground
Paying no heed to the burial mound!'

And Crispin de Quincie de Faversham-Clumps
Walked off from the funeral back to the Mumps
Back to the gargoyle and crossbow-scarred door
Young master and lord of all things that he saw

Trappings of trade and the products of power
Earth, temple, turret and brutal bell tower
Acres of panel and parquet and stair
A mass taxidermy of tiger and bear

The ghost of rough nanny's tyrannical rule
Fresh horrors in store at his murderous school
The loss and the loneliness echoing still
In the twitching of flies on the damp window sill

The whispering corridors, tarnishing hookahs
The menacing bathrooms containing verrucas
The burnt-out craft shop, the closed petting zoo
All the things that his parents intended to do

Then a clunk then a thwack, a creaking of hinge
The croaking of oak and a whistling wing
The door swung ajar and no longer alone
Poor Crispin fell into the darkness of home

To be met by old Kenilworth, buttleing still
Aged beyond reason and green at the gill
Thin as a spoke and tall as a cliff
Glaring and gartered and perfectly stiff.

Yes Kenilworth, oh such a heartening sight
Stockinged and coated as dark as the night
The dandruff cascade and the slight waft of mange
The one thing at Raddlesham never to change

'Tea in the great hall' the relic inferred
Face like a corpse and nose like a bird
With an eye on a deeply delectable worm
'Proceed, my lord Crispin, I'll stoke up the urn.'

And there in the hall that had not seen a ball
Since the very last Pujah before the great fall
From the turret of Grandpapa Jim
Who looked down from on high with his long bearded-chin.

From his frame on the wall, high but not tall
Surrounded by frames with his ancestors all
Nine generations of disparate Clumps
Nine belted knights at the seat of the Mumps.

Nine noblemen that had breathed a last breath
Whilst falling (all nine) to an untimely death.
Yes, three hundred years of the Clumps brave and bold
Now reduced to a lad only seven years old

Crispin de Quincie de Faversham-Clumps
Felt his hair stand on end, his goosing of bumps
As a whispering tone met his nose and his ear
T'was old Kenilworth, reeking of Stilton and beer

'Terribly sad how they all passed away
I suppose sir has heard what the villagers say
'As curses breed hearses and bullocks breed muck
Do the Faversham-Clumpses breed bloody bad luck.'

But I'll tell you the story just so as you know
Of how your ancestors did nobly go
Yes I'll start at the start as we've plenty of time
For the tragical chapters that number at nine

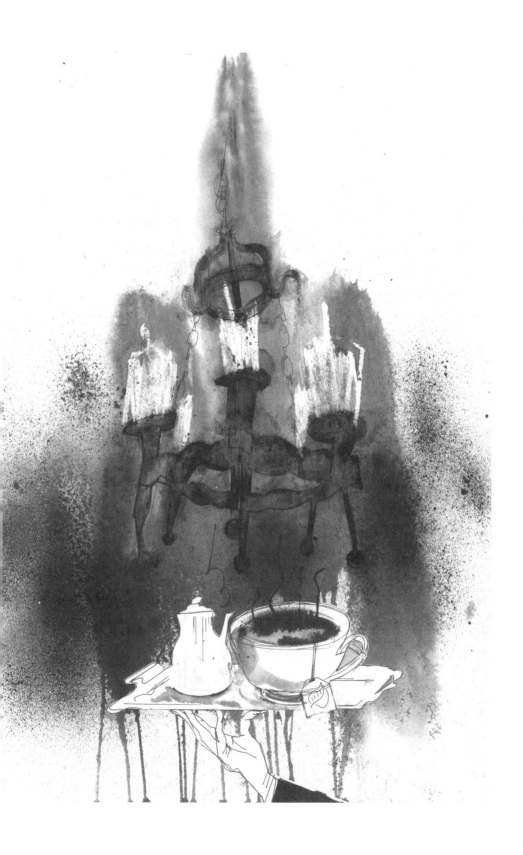

In front of the fire roaring-'n'-roasting
In front of the hounds gently ticking and toasting
Old Kenilworth served up in neat little chunks
The tale of the deaths of the Faversham-Clumps.

Act II. The deaths

1. Ocken de Fanwicke de Noggindon Clumps

Old Ocken de Fanwicke now there was a man
Broad as a bullock and firm as a ham
Busy and bellicose, whiter than lard
Won the old Mumps on the turn of a card

Brutal in taste and a lover of power
Added the west wing and built the bell tower
Ocken's desire was blood on the lip
Bare knuckle fighting a-stripped to the hip

Went to the fair ground and took to the ale
Fought a French midget and swore to prevail
Called for tobacco at round fifty five
By round sixty seven more dead than alive

The doctors were called in at round eighty-four
The Frenchman was dead and the crowd gave a roar
Ocken drank on till he fell in his bed
And the very next morning poor Ocken was dead.

2. Fossil de Fanwicke de Noggindon Clumps

Fossil de Fanwicke an elegant cove
Wore a tall hat above eyes that did rove
Added the ballroom and ladies salon
Filled it with laughter before very long

Fossil liked ladies and ladies liked he
So many ladies! Oh how could there be?
Fossil gave chase like a fox in a coupe
Hither and thither got caught in a loop

Died in the village whilst cutting a swathe
The wife of a blacksmith was seen at the grave
Proclaiming 'Here's Fossil, undoubtedly dead
By the means of the anvil what fell on his head'

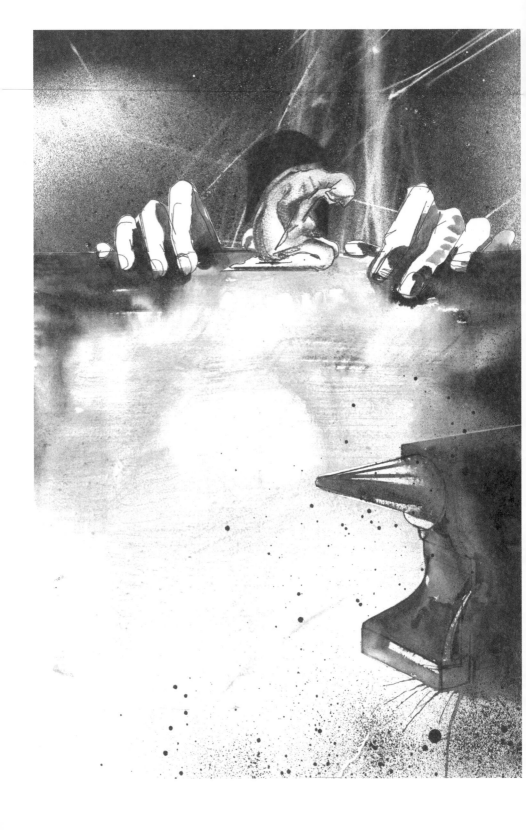

3. Enid de Bullsby de Funnlewick Clumps

Enid, ah yes, of the Funnlewick limb
Occult and mystery journeys within
Built the earth temple all wild and weird
Tattooed a pentagram under her beard

Danced with witches in green firelight
Conjured the curse with his ritual and rite
Enid danced into the hole in the hill
For all that we know she could be in there still

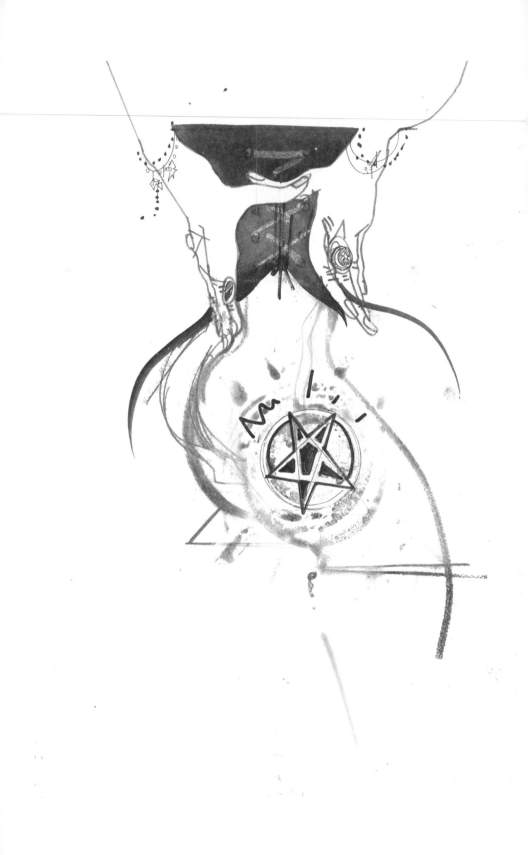

Calling aloud in the night of Soween
The promise she made to the great fairy queen.'
The words of the curse that she carved on the wall
'When the old fights the new will great Raddlesham fall'

4. Palsy de Bullsby de Funnlewick Clumps

Palsy possessed a terrific moustache
Neck and eyelashes just like a Giraffe
Went on his travels brought back a baboon
Taught it to dance to a nautical tune

Taught it to sit and eat supper at eight
Smoke a cigar and run half the estate
Put it in charge of the stocks and the shares
Said the baboon knew the bulls and the bears

Borrowed and borrowed, fell foul of the bank
Lost every penny and deeper he sank
The ape ran away with the gardener's wife
Leaving poor Palsey to take his own life

Found in the bell tower: ding a ding dong
Hadn't been hanging about very long.
Ding a ding-dong, ding a ding-dong
Hadn't been hanging about very long.

5. Cordon de Whooton de Chaddlewick Clumps

Cordon de Whooton de Chaddlewick Clumps
Garrulous 'groovy' delightfully plump
Foraging freely through forest and moor
Berry and bramble he picked by the score

Found a fine fungus of curious hue
Gobbled it down and turned indigo blue
Sang in a falsetto, befriended a bee
Told the policeman he had to be free.

Riding his tenuous grip on elation
Vaulted the fence of a large power station
Called from the roof for a crab-apple flan
Died with one bell bottom caught in a fan

6. Iffley de Wooten de Chaddlewick Clumps

Iffley, oh yes, was Grandpapa Jim
Went to Karachi and came back so thin
Brought home a guru who looked very odd
Built the great shrine to the elephant god

Grew Iffley's beard to a monstrous length
Puffed on a hookah to help with his strength
Climbed up the turret to take in the air
Some people say that he tripped on his hair.

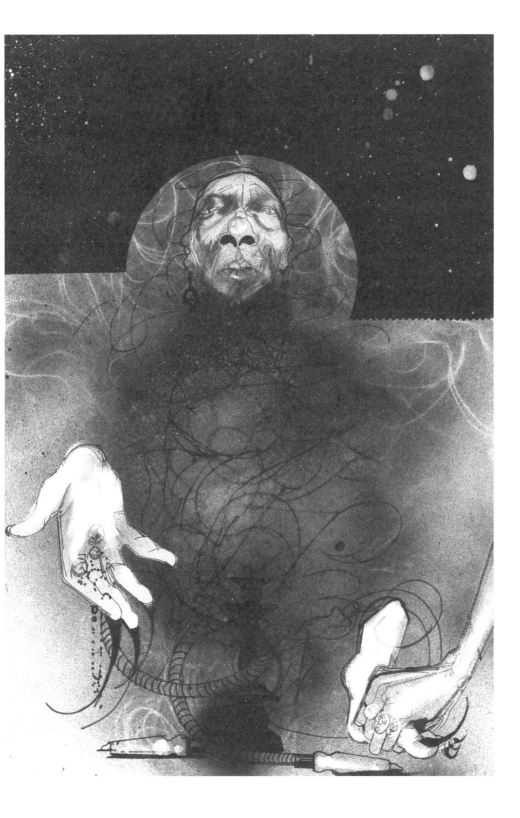

Made for a terrible site in the dusk
Impaled through his neck on an elephants tusk

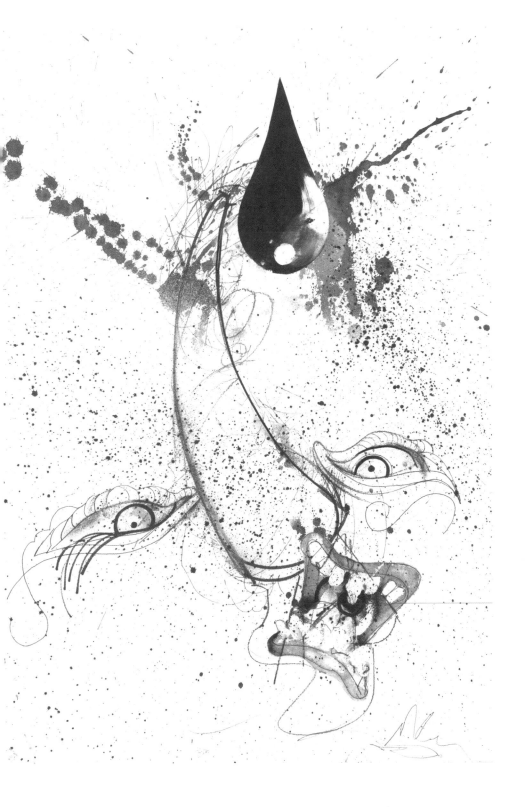

7. Noggin de Lanyard de Braddlehook Clumps

Noggin your uncle was N to the C
Noggin like funk with a capital G
Told the police he was doing his thing
Packing a Mac and some serious bling

Turned the conservatory into a club
Took a bazooka and shot at the pub
Bought a pet tiger to show to his friends
And Noggin would never be heard of again.

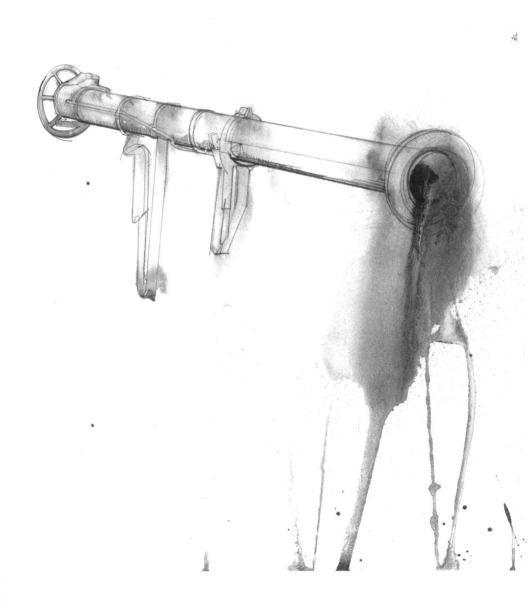

8. Hoggard de Lanyard de Braddlehook Clumps

Your father so gifted with skillet and pan
Celebrity chef with a signature flan
Businesses, businesses quickly they grew
First the farm shop then a new petting zoo

Everything packaged and cleverly branded
Feted and flannelled his ego expanded
Hoggard was swept in the media swoon
Raddlesham rose like a coloured balloon

Higher and wider and stronger and faster
Followed his path to impending disaster
His publicist told him he needed a cause
Soon he was spouting the maritime laws

Went to Antarctica, wind in his sales
Making a film about saving the whales
Preening and posing and beating his chest er
Died with a harpoon shot through his sow ester'

Act II

'And that is the story and those are the words
The number of three multiplied into thirds
Cold in their graves at the seat of the tumps
And their ghosts stalk the halls of these Raddlesham Mumps'

'What terrible luck all my ancestors had'
Young Crispin said looking the faintest bit sad
'But I counted eight and I'm sure you said nine
There's surely one more in this unhappy line'

With skeletal digit from spidery limb
Old Kenilworth gestured beyond papa Jim
A fine gilded frame hung above the great door
With the subject uncertain (the work was so poor)

'You like it?' The butler quite keenly enquired
Whilst kicking the dogs from in front of the fire
'What is it?' came Crispin's politest reply
'Look closer young master: look deep in the eye.'

The chin and the nose and the neck and the hair?
I'm sure you can guess who's residing in there
A touch of Van Dyke and a sniff of Van Gough,'
The servant affected a diffident cough

'Suppose sir would care for the portraitist's name?'
"Not really," said Crispin, "I find it quite plain
I can see it's a person: that must be an eye?
But I can't really tell where the mouth or nose lie

It's been a long day of discussing the dead
I wish to retreat to the comfort of bed."
'But master' begged Kenilworth 'Surely you see
The quite unmistakable identity . . .?'

With a cackling-laugh and a strange little dance
The centegenarion capered and pranced
'Perhaps: some more tea? 'Shall I make it for two?
For the artist me and the subject is you'

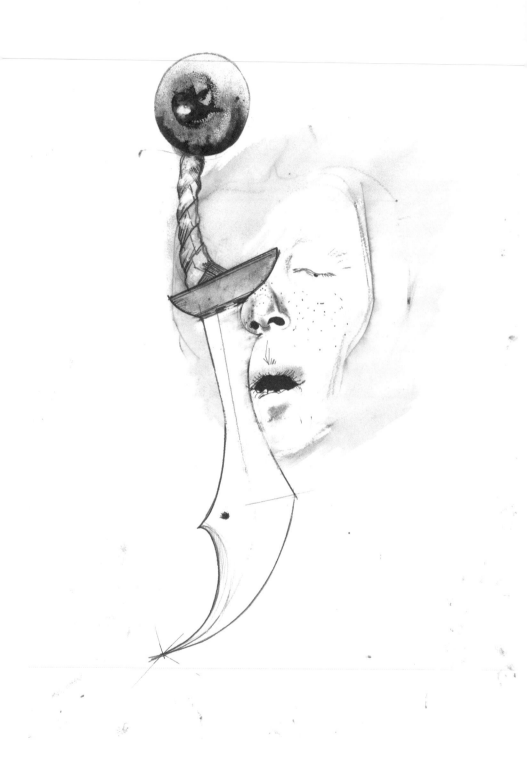

'Crispin de Quincy, quite easily lead
Found in the bell tower missing his head
Crispin de Quincy with britches of red
Terrible shame that he ended up dead'

A hideous howl from old Kenilworth's throat
Met the ears of some witches (north of the moat)
And the Raddlesham Foxes turned on their tale
At emission of such an implausible wail

'Knavery! Slavery, cruellest deceit
Stolen by him that despicable cheat
Pilfered by you and your decadent line
The Raddlesham Mumps is quite rightfully mine'

'For who came before you? Yes us! It was we
The ancient Lords of the Kenilworth tree
We cut down the trunks and we grubbed out the stumps
With the steam off our backs, built the Raddlesham Mumps'

'We watched as the Romans they came and they went
We paid to the Normans ridiculous rent
Brought Raddlesham Mumps through the coarse and the fine
It's been Kenilworth owned since the dawning of time'

'But hoodwinked we were, by the turn of a card
By Ocken, with skin, that was whiter than lard
But we paid him his dues on the night of the fight
Oh we paid him a visit deep into the night

No sooner we buried him out by the tumps
Another clumps came to the Raddlesham Mumps
But Fossil was easy to trap with his need
Enid was next metaphysical greed

Palsey, oh yes with a ding a ding dong
Whooton indeed we just pushed him along
Like ants they kept on but we bided our time
Til we duly disposed of this mongrelous line

Iffley was killed with a fabulous ruse
Noggin quite gory but oh it amused
Hoggard was last, killed the Mrs as well
And you my 'lord' Crispin – now welcome to hell!

And all of a sudden old Kenilworth changed
From manically morbid to calmly deranged
As he stood up quite straight and surveyed the great hall
And pulled down a battle-axe, hung on the wall

'Oh will you go willingly unto your grave?
Great grandson of treachery nephew of nave
I cursed at the crib on the night of your birth
But I always quite liked you for what it is worth'

And with that he swung with a swish and a whine
As the battle axe passed with margin so fine
That had Crispin been wider this book would have closed
As he smelt the warm steel as it passed by his nose

A swipe and a jump and a slash and a duck
An expletive or two (but I won't mention that)
'And now my 'young master' old Kenilworth said
My motive is simply to chop off your head'

But Crispin was quick to a lance and shield
The young and the old took their place on the field
And before very long neath the gnash and the roar
Would but one of two hearts be-a-beating no more

They battled up stair and they fought along hall
They teetered and tottered but neither would fall
From parapet, battlement, turret or tower
To smashing and crashing and chandelier shower

The pike then the poleax the club then the flail
The scythe and the spetum the helmet and mail
The parry and pivot, the lunge and the fade
The balance was perfect 'tween youth and great age

But Ocken and Fossil and Enid and Palsey
Now Wooten and Noggin and Hoggard and Iffley
Slid down from the portraits that hung on the wall
Armed to the teeth gave their rallying call

'Hoorah' called the ghosts of the Raddlesham Mumps
'Hoorah' cried the voice of ancestral Clumps
'Slay this the last dog of the Kenilworth tree
'Vengeance young Crispin before victory'

But then out from the chapel 'neath transept and nave
The Kenilworth ghosts pulled themselves from their graves
With war hammer, quarterstaff, cudgel and mace
They flew up on the Clumps at a clattering pace

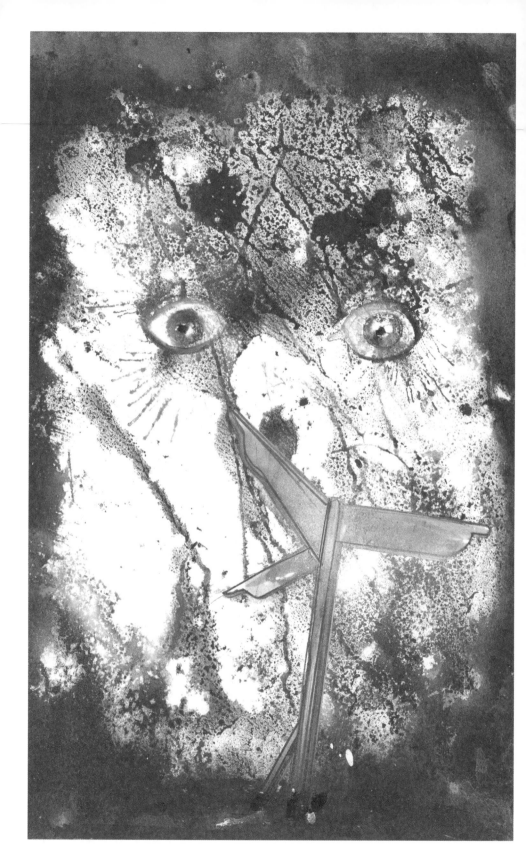

'To me!' called old Kenilworth 'Now we shall fight'
He drew himself up to his fullest of height
With flourish of hand and a masterly bearing
Calling ghost trumpets a blasting and blaring

Outside the sky darkened and darkened some more
Strange noises came calling the crow and jackdaw
The flap of the raven, the tramping of boot
The rest of the witches in time for their moot

Alighting their minibus wearing tall hats
With lotion and potion and seventeen cats
The green fire sprang neath the spreading oak tree
Whilst the witches imbibed a divine herbal tea.

Inside the fight rang as spectre and ghost
Joined the butler and boy fighting pillar to post
The wraith and the phantom the slash and the bite
The old fought the new to the depths of the night

The witches in trances danced over the mound
The green firelight lit the burial ground
To illuminate letters carved in the wall
When the old fights the young will great Raddlesham fall

Green fire leaped higher strange music called out
The witches in unison gave up the shout
'Come forth ye wee folk to the Raddlesham come
For the curse is invoked and your work must be done'

So out poured the fairy folk out from the hill
Riding dragonfly steeds with impossible skill
The Fairy Queen called them to muster and come
To the voice of the pipe and the beat of the drum

High in the sky did the fairy folk fly
As the battle played out to a murderous cry
The magical music transformed to a roar
As it blew out the windows and smashed down the door

They flew like a swarm through the Raddlesham hall
The sound beat the ground as it juddered the walls
And the parapet buttress and block
The window-frame, wattle and lever and lock

But a timorous voice called out painfully thin
Growing louder it rose to the clamorous din
'Stop, stop!' Called out Crispin. 'Please stop this now cease
I must speak; give me silence, my lords I pray peace.

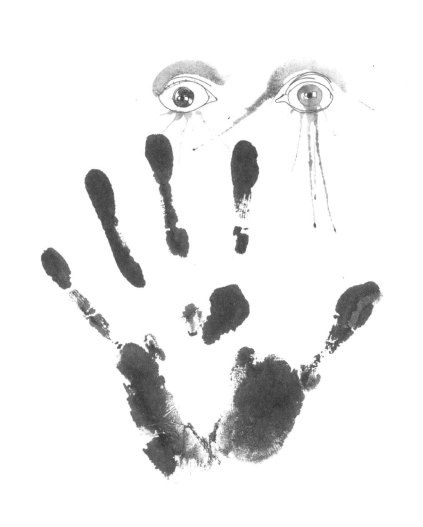

And suddenly all things decided to stop
It's said one could hear a pentameter drop
The Mumps saw a sudden cessation of play
Awaiting the weight of what Crispin would say.

'Kenilworth wishes death, I understand why
But he's too old to kill and I'm too young to die
I don't want this great house and I never did either
Its smelly and damp oh you have to believe-

Whereas Kenilworth wishes in truth to succeed
There's nothing I want here and nothing I need
I'm seven years old with no knowledge of greed
He must take it right now with the title and deed

'Mine' Said old Kenilworth 'Mine did you say?'
You'll abdicate now and walk duly away?'
'In a second' said Crispin his voice wearing thin
'The plumbing's all shot and the roof's falling in

'The heating's gone wonky the lead-work in doubt
The chimneys are singularly lacking in grout'
No friends and no family just empty beds
You've murdered them all every last one is dead'

'It's a dump and the damp is now turning to wet
I'd prefer to exist in a caravanette'
'A caravanette?' Kenilworth did repeat
'With a toilette cassette and a swivelling seat?'

'Yes I'd drive to Ibiza I'd laugh and have fun
I could swim in the sea and then lay in the sun
I might meet some new friends and relax by the pool
Far better than life with those beasts at my school

'Ibiza well, well said the centegenarion
And I suppose you'd become vegetarian?
May I suggest, with no wish to be rude
That you journey to Italy? Much better food

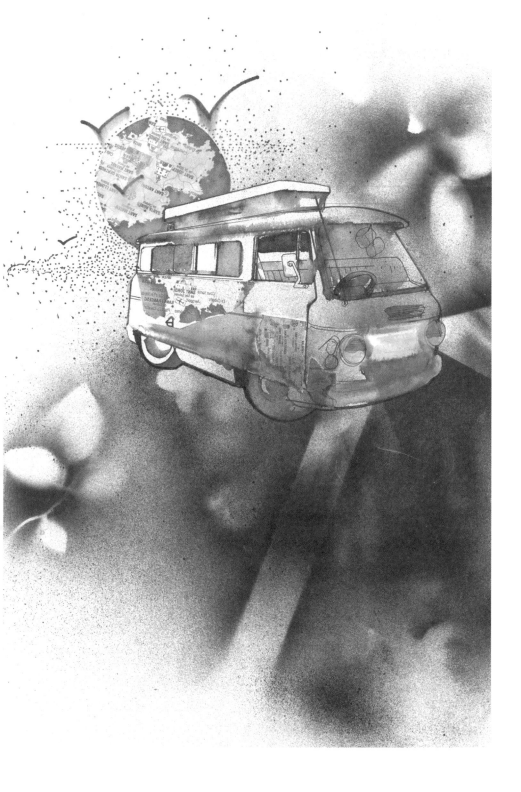

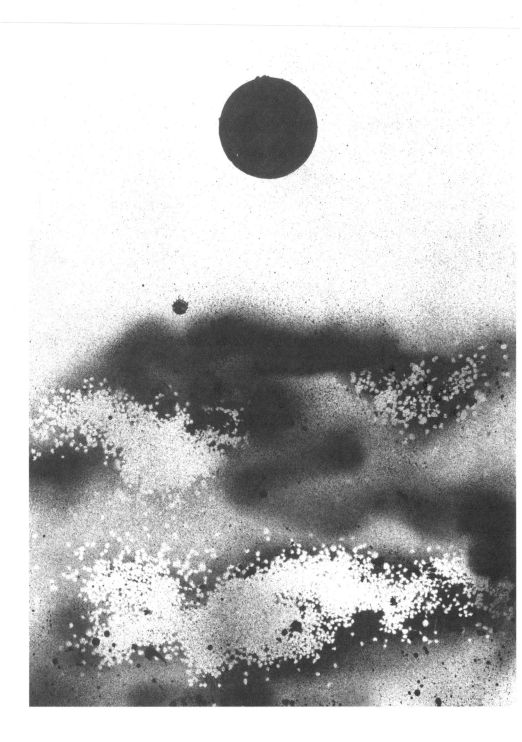

Tuscany, Puglia then to Taormina
Smell the wild sage and the lemon verbena
Capri, Ginostra then Filicudi
Brava bellissima, ragazza! Scusi!

'Maybe' said Crispin 'I'd not thought of that
But certainly I'd purchase a colourful hat'
'Well, well' declared Kenilworth 'Just fancy that
And you'd quite unequivocally never be back?'

And the fairy queen listened, as too did the host
As the dragonflies rested as well as the ghosts
And the witches outside neath the dawn treading sky
All waited upon young Lord Crispin's reply

As he looked at his ancestors up on the wall
As he looked at the hearth and the hounds and the hall
At the banner and birthright, his place in the role
His heart felt the pain in old Kenilworth's soul

'I give up my claim on the Raddlesham Mumps
I give up my seat as the lord of the Clumps
As I throw down my limb of the Raddlesham tree
I declare now the masters must Kenilworth be'

And Crispin knelt down before Kenilworth's blade
He lowered his head to the oath he had made
And the ghosts and the Fairy Queen duly did spy
A tear breach the corner of Kenilworth's eye

For that moment it seemed that all would be well
That the Mumps had averted the horrible spell
As old Kenilworth thrust out the ring on his hand
To the lips of the last to have squatted his land

He reached for the dagger kept deep in his sleeve
'Come closer young Crispin' his wish to deceive
Wrapped up soft in the tone of a gentle old man
'Let me hug you my boy' he concealed his foul plan

Grasping Crispin's blond curls in his bony embrace
Pulling up the young chin to reveal the fair face
Such a lily-white neck did his wickedness spy
That the jugular vein drew a sinister cry

'Blood' he spat 'blood, let it spill let it pour
Let it swell like an ocean across this cruel floor'
Vile dog you must perish and now is the time
To honour my word and extinguish your line'

'Prepare foolish child to breath your last breath
For I bring you no mercy, no I bring only death'
As the blade was pulled high for the cruel final blow
Kenilworth felt the rush of his victory flow

But up through the air a lone fairy pipe sang
Such a note filled with sparseness of beauty it rang
Through the hall in the sweetest of tone
Turning Kenilworth's hand as if to cold stone

Growing louder and keener and greater stronger
The Raddlesham Mumps could contain it no longer
A great crack appeared in the high vaulted hall
And a great stone dislodged and decided to fall

Down, down, down through the air its velocity grew
Kenilworth he stood still as still faster it flew
As the ghost and the host saw the stone strike his head
They agreed beyond doubt the old butler was dead

Squashed quite flat as a megrim but no guts or gore
No oceans of blood as he cruelly foresaw
Just a small cloud of steam through his clothes percalated
For nine decades of hate left him quite desiccated

But that vapour took form in that moment of still
As down Crispin's young spine shot a tingling chill
As a tall and thin ghost boy with blue lips from the cold
Who could not have been much more than seven years old

Stepped out from old Kennilworth's flattened remains
And skipped away from the Mumps to the piper's refrain
Up out past the witches who all stood there stock still
As the ghost boy danced into hole in the hill.

Now the fairy drums joined and the singers sang out
The great walls of the hall started moving about
As the buttress and balustrade lintel and stair
Started falling each time missing just by a hair

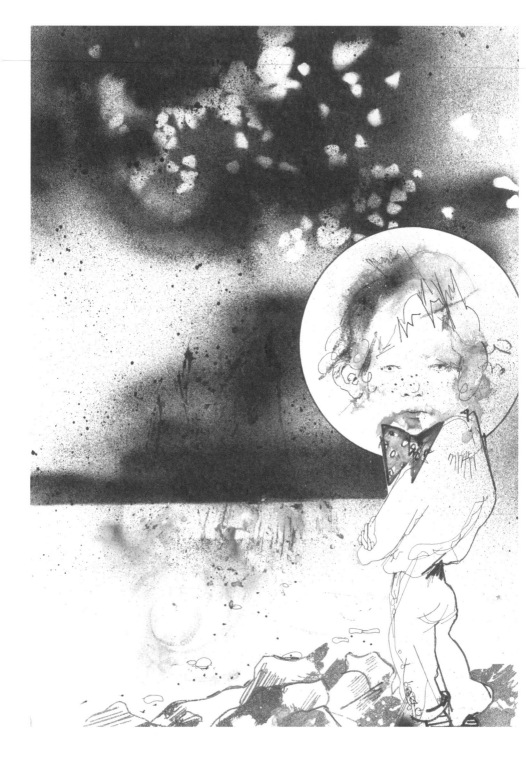

The frail form of Crispin now standing alone
In the heart of the hall of this unhappy home
But the Queen being quick leapt up fast to his need
As she rode to his aid on her dragonfly steed

And so Crispin was borne up and carried away
As the Raddlesham mumps met its sudden decay
And the ghost host was scattered and fled through the gloom
As the final block fell on old Kenilworth's tomb

And the fairy folk flew back deep under the tumps
And the green firelight saw the very last clumps:
Crispin sitting with witches there under the tree
For a cuddle, a cat and a cup of hot tea.

So now there lays the tale, my friends it is told
Make of it what you will and a lad brave and bold
Who though seven years old had the wisdom you see
That in letting things go one can set one's self free

And if to the isle of Ibiza you stray
Why not keep your eyes open for maybe one day
You will notice a man in a colourful hat
In a caravanette with an old witch's cat

And a smile on his face and a laugh in his eye
On a chain round his neck: a fine gold dragonfly

THE END

About the Author

Murray Lachlan Young is a poet, broadcaster and stand-up performer. He came to prominence during the Brit Pop era of the mid-1990s, when he became the only poet to sign a contract worth £1m. His work echoes the great rhymers Edward Lear, Lewis Carrol and Gilbert and Sullivan, along with more alternative influences such as Grandmaster Flash, Tom Waits and Ian Dury. His satirical commentaries range from the vanities of celebrity and middle-class angst, to highlighting the absurdities of modern life.

Today Murray is best known as an 'across networks' performer on BBC radio. He has been commissioned by Mark Rylance to commemorate the Globe theatre's relocation to its current home, by BBC World Service to explore the connection between science and religion for a special program recorded at CERN in Switzerland, and he co-wrote the 2015 film adaptation of Dylan Thomas' *Under Milk Wood*. Murray has two sons and now lives in London.